Gordon Delfino

„Damn you Autocorrect - The Brandnew Top 50 Auto Correct Fails"

Aniqy Publishing
77 Oxfordstreet London
United Kingdom

ISBN-13:
978-1480087835

ISBN-10:
1480087831

Damn You Auto Correct
The Brandnew Top 50 Auto Correct Fails!

AutoCorrect makes you look pretty stupid sometimes.

People texting a word but their phones auto correct feature suddenly has a mind of ist own. So its Randomly correcting words incorrectly!

You like texting humor, or taking just a little bit of pleasure in the misfortune of others? This book will leave you laughing until the end!

You will find my Top 50 of AutoCorrect in this book!

Gordon Delfino

LAID THE BABYSITTER

„Did you guys eat dinner yet?"

„Yep. Just had pasta... Oh by the way, i laid the babysitter."

„Uh, excuse me? You fucking what?"

„Haha PAID. I paid her. Sorry to give you a heart attack babe"

„I hate you! :)"

THE FÜHRER

„Don't worry, seriously. He's crazy about you and he loves you so much. He told me the other day that you're the first girl he had ever thought about the führer with."

„What?????"

„Ok so that supposed to say future… Damn iPhone!"

R A P E . . .

„Ha I meant to say lawn don't know how the fuckbucket that turned into yaks"

„Lol, so you're dad can't pick me up?"

„No I'll send a yak and you can rape it here"

„RIDE !!!"

„LMFAO.. What were you trying to say?"

„Ride a yak to my horn"

DICKHEALER

„Uncle dickhealer wants you poppin checkin grandpa when you get done with whore"

„?????"

„None of this was right at all. Uncle denny wants you to stop and check on grandpa when you get done with work"

TOUCH BALLS

„Will you let Richard know that I just now finished my last day of community service!!!! And, that I will call him tomorrow and touch balls with him about Friday."

„Shit! I meant base but coudn't stop it in time."

„I am about to cry"

„From sadness or my mistake?"

„From hysterical laughter"

FELLATIO

„Are you free? Wanna come over tonight for cards and fellatio"

„OMG. That was supposed to say gelato"

„Well, at first I was all fo it, but then....."

PENIS

„i just got in a huge fight with a co worker"

„Why? What happened? Are you ok?"

„stupid really... i needed a penis and he wouldn't let me borrow one"

„What??????!!!"

„oh I'm going to throw this stupid phone in the trash. I needed a pen"

TICKLING COPS

„she got in her car and was sitting in the driveway for about 5 mins and he walked out there to tell her to leave and she threw a coke at him and said I'm calling the tickling cops"

„Maby you should call the tickling cops they sound fun like jist the thing to break up the stressful mood."

„Lol right tickling cops.. :) I wonder if they come in those shiny plastic leather suits and blare its raining men with feather dusters"

OPRAH WINFREY

„Guess whos black!!"

„Um... I don't know... Oprah Winfrey??"

„Haha I meant : Guess whos back! Because i'm back from Austin"

„Good to know! Now let's go dwarfing"

CHICKEN VAGINAS

„Chicken vaginas sound good for dinner ?"

„No... not really."

„What would you rather have?"

„Definitely not chicken vaginas"

„laugh, Chicken fajitas... stupid autocorrect"

„oh... that sounds much better :)"

TUCKING

„What you doin?"

„Fucking my dog in bed"

„Oh god oh go! Do not read that!"

„TUCKING!"

„i meant tucking my dog in bed!"

„The T is close to the F on this thing.."

„Sorry!"

POOP PARTY

„You missed a good BBQ"

„There is a poop party on the 18th august"

„Pool!"

„cool"

„i'll put that in my calender"

DADDY DOG

„I love thunder so much"

„i know me too! Except when it makes my dog bark., so usually only when I'm outside"

„My dad barks too, we have to comfort him"

„Im so sorry, I imagine his manly vocal chord cause much more commotion than a small dog"

„laugh, Oh did you mean dog?"

„yeah no duh..."

SHUCKING

„Whats up?"

„Not much. I've just been sucking penis all day"

„Thats good for you"

„oh dear god.. shucking peanuts"

„piece of shirt phone"

ORANGE HIV

„Anything from Mc Donalds ?"

„Ohh yes please! 5 pice hicky select meal medium with organs"

„Hahaha. Chicken select with orange HIV"

„Ewww what kind of organs?"

„Dammit, Hi C "

„No AIDS?"

„i hate you"

PEANUT BASTARD PRAIFATE

„What would you like from dairy queen?"

„I want one of those peanut bastard praifate"

„Really now? I don't think they have those"

„Yes they do. peanut busted parfeetp"

„Yeah they don't have those either"

„ok so my typing skills suck. Peanuts betters parfait to..."

YANKING OIL

„Bring some yanking oil"

„Some WHATTT ????"

„Tanning oil, bring some tanning oil!! What kind of word is yanking ... haha"

„Please don't bring your KY!! lol! Thats good shit!!

„Laughing so hard I'm crying!! And trying to explain to your dad why!!"

BURNING NUNS

„only if there are no puppet people near."

„lol. It's so hot. Like there are a thousand burning nuns in the sky."

„I don't know you'd launch that many nuns into the sky. Especially if they are on fire."

„What?"

„I dunno. You're the one burning nuns."

„Damn phone. SUNS. Not nuns. Lol!

PUSSY WAND

„Highly probable it is.."

„Haha thank you yoda."

„Haha welcome you are young pussy wand"

„LMAO"

„What??"

„Please tell me that was intentional"

„i tried typing padawan..."

BITE MY BALLS

„What do you do when you're nervous?"

„crack my knuckels and used to bite my balls bit not any more"

„Hahahaha...."

„Opps meant my nails... haha"

„Ok that imagine i could that"

„i will never let you live that one down"

„i figured as much"

PENIS ATTACK

„Morning babycakes! xo"

„Worst night ever"

„Aww why??"

„Woke up with penis attack and diarreah"

„OMG"

„Panic attack.... i think i ate a bad dick"

„ugh dinner"

„i like the idea of a penis attack better!"

GRANDMOTHER

„Gardening can be healing"

„Or at least fun"

„I love it so does Bekka"

„I just did my Grandma hard!"

„OMG"

„Ohhh .. I just did my grandmothers yard.."

„Autocorrect. I Swear"

„We know you saucy boy, are you that lonely?"

DOCK

„Dan and I are going out. dinners in the microwave."

„awesome! your the best! where you heading?"

„he's going to show me his cock!! im super excited!!"

„WWTF mom ewww why would you say that?"

„OMG!! his COCK!"

„yeah got it mom .. thanks!"

„stupid phone D O C K, where he keeps his boat!"

„yeah ok"

„excuse me????"

„im telling dad!"

ASSHOLE SAUCE

„ok good. I'll make that with some mashed potatoes and stuffing... and i got cinnamon asshole sauce"

„Wowwww Cinnamon asshole sause????? Ouch?!"

„OMG not asshole sauce... apple sauce!"

„I'm dying over here lol"

„That got kinky real fast"

COOCH

„Damn I want a new cooch my cooch is getting worn down any suggestions?"

„Auto correct?"

„lol"

„Damn it"

CORK

„Show that turd who is boss!"

„I farted right when you sent that .. yummm."

„Nice work. A fart is just a turd honking for the right of way."

„waaaaahhhhhhhh"

„Put a cock in it."

„CORK !!!!"

DEAR DEAD

„What are your plans for today then??"

„Nothing beyond seeing you dead xx"

„DEAR !!!! Damn auto correct!!!!"

HORSEDICK

„I'm good. This pregnancy is giving me massive cravings for horsedick"

„OMG"

„Horseradish, Horseradish, Horseradish..... !!!!!!"

„Stop it... hahahahha"

PNEUMONIA

„Yoko One sounds horrible"

„Lol I typed pneumonia"

„But auto correct is actually correct"

WHORE MILK

„Can I ask you a favor of u"

„what would that be, going back to work in about 20 minutes"

„After work can u bring home a 4 litter of white whore milk we are out and I'm craving it badly"

„White whore milk? Not sure where to get that but I'll try :p"

„Hahaha duck i ment white homo milk"

„Fuck not duck... shit"

T W A T

„Lol... Chewy bacon is the best.. Mmmmm"

„I like to crack in my twat"

„oh my gosh"

„teeth"

„Loool"

„I do not put bacon in my twat"

„Wow. Obviously apple believes you like to use some interesting words..."

IN THE CAT

„Aww traffic is really bad now.. I don't wanna be in the cat anymore..."

„Aw I wouldn't want to be inside a cat either!"

„XD"

FRENCH GIRL

„How did things go with the french girl?"

„Went really bad she wasn't interested I ended up killing her sister in the barn next to her house"

„Oh my god, hat happend???"

„Kissing ha ha... auto correct"

„Spastic!!!"

VAPORIZED

„Cousin night?"

„Denny is getting vaporized, so I'll be at church."

„Babtized"

SHARTBREADS

„Are you coming home soo? Picking up food on your way? We have no food except shartbreads and i can't eat any more of thme , they are giving me heartburn"

„Shartbreads? That doesn't sound appetizing..."

„I meant shartbreads"

„Omg why does my phone want to say that????"

„DYAC"

„Short breads!!"

NEED A NAP

„I need anal. But I can't just take one for 15 minutes like eric. I have to have like 2 hours, so it never happens. :("

„haha what?"

„Wow iPhone really? Forget one space and now my husband is gay and I'm a freak."

„I need a NAP! hahaha"

„Hahaha I wasjust thinking omg!"

SHITSTAIN

„Happy mothers day shitstain .. luv luv xoxo"

„OMG I meant sweetness! Way to ruin your day, huh?."

„I love you!"

„Shitstain.... hahaha! Well happy mothers day to u too fuckface...lol.. Love u too"

„touché"

MISSED CALL

„Hey sorry I missed you're call... what's up?"

„Hold on one second I am fucking your brother in bed"

„Ew. Mom?! WTF?"

„Ohh sorry I menat tucking... This darn phone!"

„..."

MOMS ASS

„I didn't even get those msgs lol. It was a parking ticket for parking onur moms ass. Made me so mad.."

„Wait no.. Auto correct!"

„U of M's grass!"

„My mpms ass!!! Braddddd!!!! "

„Im sorry. That was a terrible autocorrect! Yeah if i parked there I prob would have goten a big ticket. And arrested!"

FLYING SQUIRTS

„D I caught sme squirts!"

„Thats nice, I guess."

„Yea, you want one?"

„Ummm, no thanks. You can keep'em.

„You sure? They're the flying ones.."

„Lane... Flying squirts?! Why would I want that?!"

„SQUIRRELS!"

„Bahahahaa! I thought you were sick or something."

LESBIAN

„1 more beer then we're lesbian..."

„i knew it"

„Ewww WTF?"

„Autocorrect!!!! Haha!! Leaving!!!"

BLOW UP FRIEND

„Oh it's ok, I went to sleep on the blow up mistress"

„read what u just sent!"

„Ugh blow up MATTRESS.. lol Stupid auto correct!!"

„Sorry mom"

„Lol I knew what you meant. Didn't think u had a blow up friend...."

„Lol!! That's too funny! Hahaha!! Swear I meant mattress, no blow up mistresses here.. lol"

NEW IPHONE

„Hey Mommy do you like your new iPhone? I love mine!"

„Hey dingleberry yeah it's gret I lobster all the fetish. Much llamas to you from dad"

„Mom??"

„Opss how do I tell off erection?"

„How do i tell off Autocorrect?"

„...."

TIRED

„You naked yet?"

„What the heck!!!!!?"

„Meant to say tired yet! Stupid Phone changed the word!!"

RAVING

„I may eat my arm! I'm starving! What time are you leaving?"

„I'm getting raising canes!"

„Raving at 6.00 Please get me some too!! I'll pay you back"

„I will! How Manu"

„Opp! Leaving.. not ravng. Ha! However many you get - it's good leftover"

„Yeah and many not Manu! Ha!

ONE ERECTION

„Duh! :D"

„lol allrighty there"

„Lol yeppers samon brain"

„Fishy don't call me that"

„I smell something fishy coming from maklaya"

„I smell a piggy coming from Morgans erection"

„direction!"

„Lmaoooo"

HORRIBLE WEATHER

„That the weather was being suck a prick!"

„Such"

„LMAO!!!"

„Whose home are you at?"

„Damn you autocorrect!"

„Can tell what phrase your phone is used to!!"

TO EARLY FOR THAT

„Good. Cake?"

„To early for that. I think I'll have cervical instead"

„shit!!! Cereal!!"

„Bahahahaha"

„I meant CEREAL"

„Omg I didn't see what you typed first. Best auto correct!"

MONEY TALKS

„I'll just have to buy another.. I guess"

„I can get you one for a super cheap on ebay"

„I'll get it :) its no big deal.."

„No seriously I can get you one for like 99 cunts"

„99 cunts?????"

„how do you pay in cunts?"

„i meant cents!! oh gosh"

VIRGIN

„They added a 13th zodiac sign so now everyone is a different sign."

„They can't do that"

„Too late! They did. It was on the news."

„I'm still a virgin""

„Lol you said : I'm still a virgin"

„Damn, VIRGO"

Made in the USA
San Bernardino, CA
18 December 2018